Animals

. . . .

Contents

What is an animal?

An **animal** is a **living** thing.

A bear is an animal.

wings

A bird is an animal.

fin   fin

A fish is an animal.

tail

A lizard is an animal.

wings

An insect is an animal.

What do animals look like?

Where do animals live?

fly

hop

swim

How do animals move?

What do animals need?

Animals **need** food.

Animals need water.

Animals need air.

Animals need **shelter**.
Animals need **space**, too.

How do animals grow?

egg

frog

tadpole

adult

Animals **change** and **grow**.

Whose baby
am I?